Surviving the First Year of College
Myth vs. Reality

Steve Gladis, Ph.D.

HRD Press ❖ Amherst ❖ Massachusetts

Published by: HRD Press, Inc.
22 Amherst Road
Amherst, MA 01002
800-822-2801 (U.S. and Canada)
413-253-3488
413-253-3490 (fax)
www.hrdpress.com

Printed in Canada

Dedication

To my extraordinary daughters,
Jess and Kimberly

Table of Contents

Introduction

As a parent and a college professor, I observed students over the years as they attempted to navigate the oftentimes rough waters of their first year in college. Some were successful, others not so. I began informally to collect my observations of their voyages through the first year in the hope that I could help future students make the transition more easily.

The project of actually writing down these observations for surviving the first year began several years ago when a friend of mine asked that I talk to her son about how to survive his first year of college. Like any good parent, she wanted to protect her son and her investment...though her son's future success by far eclipsed her monetary concerns.

So, I decided to write a letter to Brian. In this letter, I gave him ten steps to survive the first year of college. Not knowing if he would take such unsolicited advice seriously, I later asked his mother about his reaction. She said that he really appreciated the tips and had even thumbtacked the letter to the bulletin board in his room. Later I found that he had taken it to college to mount on his dorm wall. That surpassed my expectations–I was pleased to learn that anything I had written was read, and more than once!

Then something strange happened. Brian's mother told other parents about the letter. Many of them asked for a copy for their sons or daughters, who like Brian were heading off to college, or for others who were already in their first year and in need of some straight talk. She quickly became an informal publisher for the letter, and over the past two years she has slipped copies into the hands of many anxious parents.

To test its broader appeal, I offered my letter for publication in *The Washington Post*. They published it in a special Education Section supplement. The response from readers has been gratifying. Parents have lauded it, kids have commented on its accuracy, and educators have asked permission to post the article in their classrooms, reprint it for newsletters, and even publish it on-line. In short, it has received a warm welcome in Washington, D.C.

This has encouraged me to reach out even farther. Now, I want this guide to have a wider audience because although all parents try to tell their children how to survive, and thrive, in college, few children listen—after all, what do parents know? This booklet can be the next best thing.

Foreword

Getting Started: Myth vs. Reality

The world is full of myths—common ideas that exist but are not true. Unfortunately, often such myths rule what we do and dominate our behavior. Myths can cause disorganized thinking and set up a system of behavior that is based on misconceptions and doomed to failure.

Let me give you an example of how this works. Consider the teenage girl with poor self-esteem who has accepted the myth that college is just for "smart kids." For whatever reasons, she's convinced that she's not smart. Over time, these attitudes will begin to pervade her thought process, and she will convince herself of the hopelessness of her situation. Eventually, she will begin to act in an inferior way, select unchallenging courses and perform poorly in high school. In essence, she will act out the myth—and fail to go to college.

Such destructive myths come from various sources. Some originate with kids themselves, either as defense mechanisms to cover for past or future failures or as ego boosters for successful kids who like the idea of making college sound difficult. In short, we often don't know the specific sources of myths or the motivation behind them.

This book does not pretend to be anything more than a guide designed to steer students away from the *myths* and toward the *realities* of how to survive the first year of college.

Myth #1
I'll start studying when school starts.

"Hey, I just finished four years of high school, and I need a rest."

"I went to a good school. I'm ready for college."

"Summer is for fun, not school."

"I got A's and B's in my college prep courses."

"September is for school, not July."

"Enough already with the studying."

"I need a break or my head will explode."

Reality #1
Start training now, like an athlete.

Can you imagine an athlete who wanted to qualify for the Olympics but absolutely refused to train for three months before the Olympic trials?

Outrageous.

No one would take such an athlete seriously. However, that's what most students who graduate from high school do to prepare for the biggest academic event of their lives thus far: College. They work very hard for four years: Study, take tests, take PSAT's, SAT's, and even expensive preparation courses. They take gifted-and-talented and AP courses, visit and apply to a number of universities, sweat out the acceptance process, get accepted, and graduate from high school. Then they promptly quit training for three or four months. Some students have been known to quit studying as soon as they get accepted to a college. They take on the I'm-on-board attitude, the I-don't-have-to-sweat-it-now attitude.

Wrong.

Getting in shape and staying in shape is as vital to your academic fitness as it is to your physical fitness. You can't just turn it off and on like a switch. A slow and steady pace wins this race.

This is about the toughest suggestion to self-impose. It requires the most personal discipline, and frankly, not all students can or will do this. But I guarantee that those who have the fortitude to do so will succeed.

☑ Survival Tips:

1. **Set up regular study hours.** By now you may be saying to yourself, "This guy is nuts if he thinks I'm studying regularly in the summer, when I didn't even do that during the year." OK. But if you take even as little as one hour a day and devote it to keeping the blade sharpened, it will yield great results. In fact, this is a great idea to remember: Small changes can result in big wins. Look at pro golfers and pro athletes in general. The person who loses a tournament is not dramatically worse, just a small fraction, but that makes a huge difference.

2. **Read—choose anything, but read something.** There's an ad that occasionally shows on TV that says, "Reading is fundamental." Remember that ad and act accordingly. Your reading will determine much of your success or failure in college. Many students don't enjoy reading; so, they do less and less of it. Learn to enjoy it, and you'll read more and increase your reading effectiveness. It's a simple but inevitable, progressive process. Start by reading whatever you like. I don't care if it's soup labels, comic books, short stories, or cowboy novels: Read. As you read more, your interests will broaden; the progressive process will happen naturally—trust me.

3. **Start keeping a daily calendar**. Poor time manage-
    ment causes some of the worst problems students have
    in college. During class discussions my students always
    stress this point. Here's the problem: In college you'll
    have what seems like loads of time. You may only
    average three or four hours of class a day. So it seems
    like there's time to burn. Also, it's unstructured
    time–the type that slips through your fingers like sand.
    However, the projects and homework assigned in
    college are much more substantial than those in high
    school, with virtually no oversight by teachers or
    parents. The combination of unstructured time and
    larger projects proves disastrous for the first-year
    students who don't keep a calendar and schedule their
    work.

    This problem is not limited to students in college.
    In fact, one of the hottest professions in the workforce
    is project management. Buy yourself a monthly
    calendar. Monthly ones work best because you can
    "see" one month ahead. Weekly calendars are too short-
    sighted. I suggest you practice setting up milestones and
    timelines for simple projects this summer. Write them
    on the calendar. Just get used to using it before you're
    in the middle of the first semester wondering how in the
    world you'll ever survive.

4. **Write constantly.** Runners know that to make it
    through a race, they have to develop their wind. Simply

put, they have to practice running to be ready for the race. So it is with writing. If you don't write regularly, you lose the edge, the confidence, the fluency. Start by keeping a daily journal. Buy yourself a spiral notebook, or my personal favorite, one of those black-and-white marble-covered composition books you used in elementary school. But begin writing. Start with your random thoughts. What you think about what's going on around you: Your hopes, fears, and dreams. Like reading, it doesn't matter what you write, only that you write regularly. Like reading, writing is a fundamental of college life. You'll get far more writing assigned in college than you did in high school.

The other effect of keeping a journal is that if you read what you've written, you'll find it a great way to sort out where you're headed. Your writing will reveal what's going on inside your head. Writing can be a sounding board, like a friend who listens to your inner-most thoughts. The journal is the best way I know to build up your writing wind.

Myth #2
I can afford to skip a class or two.

"I'll get a friend to take notes for me."

"If I leave early, I'll get a jump on the weekend."

"I never get anything out of class when I do go."

"I need the extra sleep much more than the class."

"That jerk doesn't deserve my attendance."

"I'll reward myself for my birthday."

Reality #2
You must attend all classes.

Woody Allen once said, "Showing up is 88 percent of life." Let me adapt that for college: Attendance is 95 percent of college academic life. If you skip class for one of a hundred excuses you may fabricate, you lose...every time. Recently a student came to me with a partial assignment saying that he didn't know about the additional requirement that had been announced in class for the past two weeks straight. My response was, "Whose fault is that?" No more discussion. You simply cannot get the information or assignments straight if you're off playing touch football, catching a movie, or just sleeping in.

What happens when you miss a class? Several things:

- *You miss assignments and amendments to assignments*. Teachers must amend projects by the very nature of academics: information changes, equipment is not available, stuff happens. In any case, you have to be there to get the scoop.

- *You get behind.* Even if someone takes notes for you, you fall behind. It's tough enough to under-stand your own notes two or three days after you've taken them—unless you review them soon after you take them. After a while you slowly but surely slip so far behind that you'll never catch up. It's a slippery slope, and it's hard to climb back up once you've slid down.

- *You project an I-don't-give-a-damn attitude to the professor.* Trust me. Professors notice the no-shows and give no breaks to students who skip class. NONE. Think about it. Professors take their subjects seriously. They spend years preparing and researching to qualify to teach. And then students skip class with no more excuse than it was a great day to sleep in or to get an early start on the weekend. Professors notice the no-shows.

   Just the opposite message comes through when you do make it to class. You show that you're concerned, dedicated, and ready to learn. In fact, it's been my experience that if a student makes the attempt by being there for every class, turning in all the assignments, and by calling or stopping by for extra help, I will go the extra mile or two to help. Most teachers I know are in the profession to help people. But we can only help those who are available and willing to meet us halfway.

☑ Survival Tips:

1. **Set a 100/100 percent show-up goal.** Make it your goal to show up to 100 percent of your classes 100 percent of the time. Begin with that fixed in your mind. Put everything else in second place, right from the first day on campus. School is your primary job. If you were to miss work every time you thought it was a nice day or whenever you had a headache, or–you fill in the excuse–think about how long it would take your boss to fire you. Go for perfect attendance. It sounds like an elementary school concept, but believe me, it's critical. But, if you *must* miss a class, consider the following tips:

2. **Communicate with the professor.** Call, e-mail, or send a note with a friend if you're sick. Sounds kind of goofy? Maybe, but it makes an impression. Again, it sends an important message: "I care enough to let you know I am on the injured list, but I'm still on the team." Again, use e-mail, phone, fax, or personal note, but make sure you try.

3. **Ask two people for their notes.** This may sound like overkill to you, but it's not. As I mentioned before, it's hard enough interpreting your own notes, let alone someone else's. By getting copies from two classmates, you're more likely to piece together what actually happened.

4. **Double check about assignments or handouts.** Be absolutely sure that you check with two classmates or the professor about any handouts given out in the class you missed. Also, check on whether any new assignments were given, or if modifications/ clarifications were made. I've found that this is one area where students constantly fumble. While they get the notes, they often forget to ask for handouts or special instructions. Usually, the result is that you may turn in a project only partially completed and receive a poor grade.

5. **Audio tape, if permitted.** To get 100 percent recall of a class you missed, audio taping is the best way. Asking a friend to tape a class you'll miss is a bit burdensome, but very useful. You (or your friend) must check with the instructor first. Don't tape without the professor's permission. Some teachers don't like being taped. Most will not care.

By the way, I have found that taping classes even when you are there, especially for those classes where you're having trouble, is a great idea. My daughter did that in college and found that taping supplemented her notes and helped her studying tremendously. But remember: Always ask permission first.

Myth #3
Only the subject material matters.

"The subject is the only lesson I have to learn."

"Teachers are all alike."

"Keep focused on the objectives and the rest will fall into place."

"Who gives a damn what she thinks."

"Screw him. I do my work and that's all that counts."

"She's not my boss; she's just a teacher."

"I'll do what I want, when I want."

"It's a free country."

Reality #3
Study the professor as well as the subject.

Let's begin with two simple, but important truths: First, people are different; and, second, professors are people. Try never to forget these two truths as you go through your first year of college.

Take the first truth: People are different. You know intuitively that this is accurate if you've ever had a family, friends, or more to the point, roommates. I'll use roommates as an example. In August prior to the start of your first year, seemingly normal people suddenly invade your life and turn into monsters within a month, a week, and in some cases, a day.

Let's examine just a few of the ways that people are different. Some people are shy and quiet. They like being alone or with one or two good friends. They enjoy, even revel, in their privacy. They actually recharge their personal energy when alone. On the other hand, other people are gregarious and enjoy being with people. They hate quiet and dislike being alone. Being around people recharges their energy level, and the more people the better. But, put a gregarious sort with a privacy lover as roommates, and sparks may fly.

Next, let me talk about people who are what I call get-it-done-now people. They love making to-do lists and scratching things off them. They were born to organize the world. While you're out at the library, they rearrange the room. They're human alarm clocks and must be early by an hour for everything. On the other hand, there are the hey-what's-the-rush people. Time for them is a relative measure. They use a sundial for a watch, if they even own a watch. They don't mind being late as long as they're having fun. "Surprise," "fun," "chill-out" are their favorite words—words that can drive the more workaholic get-it-done crowd bananas.

So far we've not even talked about all the other variables like ethnic backgrounds, multicultural differences, socioeconomics, you name it…. Actually, it's a wonder that any two people get along.

In fact, often the people we like the best are people who think and act like us. I call this "falling in love with the mirror." This isn't healthy because you close yourself off from a wide world of options and limit your ability to understand others and effectively operate in our diverse world. Treating people as if they were all the same, by ignoring their differences and approaching life and school based on only your preferences, can lead to real personality clashes, and ultimately disaster.

In short, people are different. Respect it and deal with it.

The second truth: Professors are people. When I was in college, I had no idea where my professors lived or if they had families or lives outside of school. For all I knew, they were all locked in a vault each evening and then unleashed on Monday to feed on us poor students during the day. Not so.

They too have personalities as well as ethnic, social, economic, and political differences—just like you. Some are shy, others gregarious; some are serious, others more fun-loving; some are old, others young. The list of attributes is long.

Your task is to adjust to them—not for them to adjust to you. This isn't easy. You are responsible for learning their styles and accommodating to them, not the reverse.

Above all, remember that people are different and that professors are people.

 Survival Tips:

1. **Discover your own personality**. Sit down and take an inventory of yourself. You may not have ever done this before. Figure out your preferences: Things you like. By inference, the opposite of what you like will likely give you fits. Consciously knowing your likes and dislikes is a strong start in getting to know and understand others. Remember that you will tend to like people almost immediately who share your preferences and values–people just like you. Be careful that you don't ignore the rest of the world in the process.

2. **Read the syllabus closely for hints.** See if there are any significant hints like: "strong class participation is a must," or "10 points off per day for a late paper," or "all work must be accompanied by an outline." Each instruction gives you insight into the person. For example, "strong participation" indicates a gregarious teacher who values strong social interaction. The teacher who takes off 10 points per day for late work is likely a get-it-done-now person.

3. **Talk to other students who have had the professor before.** Nothing beats experience. Interview former students and ask them about the professors, their likes and dislikes. Become a bit of a researcher. See if their answers are consistent. For example, if they all tell you

the teacher likes documentation in term papers to be exact, then you know where to place emphasis when you prepare a paper. If you get consistent information, it's likely to be true.

4. **Ask questions in class.** Better to ask up front than have a big surprise down the line…at your expense. Ask if there is a late penalty, how important documentation is, and similar questions. Teachers would rather you ask than assume. If the class is huge and you're a bit embarrassed, then schedule time for office hours and have your questions ready to go.

5. **Assume all professors are human**. It may seem ridiculous and redundant to have to say this, but so many students see professors as aloof and not of this world. Like you, they have families, likes, dislikes, good and bad days. They too pay rent, buy groceries, and lose loved ones. In short, they have the same daily pressures and issues going on in their lives that you do. Don't expect that they won't act and react like humans.

Myth #4
I can do it myself.

"Self-reliance. That's essential."

"I'll go it alone."

"If you want anything done right, do it yourself."

"If I get any help, it's like cheating."

"Me, I can trust. Others, I'm not so sure."

"If I do it, I know I can depend on it."

"Independence is a virtue."

"I'll pull myself up by my own bootstraps."

Reality #4
Form study groups to survive.

To illustrate to my classes how groups almost always outperform individuals, I ask one student to choose a letter of the alphabet randomly. Let's say the letter chosen is "S." Then I ask three people to leave the room and work together to come up with names of singers whose last names begin with "S." The rest of the class works independently. I predict that the group of three outside the room will outperform anyone left in the class. Guess what? I always win because, in fact, the small group outperforms any individual in the class by almost 3 to 1.

There has been a significant amount of communications research done on small-group performance. Small groups consist of three to five people convened to focus on an issue. Groups of two, dyads, lack the power of groups of three or more. On the other hand, groups of five or more become unwieldy.

Small groups outperform individuals because:

- *Small groups generate more options while brainstorming.* This process fosters many ideas to be generated as quickly as possible.

- *Small groups can better evaluate ideas.* Groups correct misinformation, bias, erroneous assumptions, and the like.

- *Group decisions enhance harmony.* They are
  essential where there is buy-in required after the
  session, such as choosing a correct solution that all
  must live with after the decision is made.

Small groups will almost always win. However, in an
emergency where you need a quick decision, you're
probably better off making a decision yourself. In that case,
groups might slow the process down to the point that the
decision is too late. Also, in cases where expertise counts
and you have an expert, then often the expert will outperform the group.

But if you're studying a subject and need encourage-
ment, support, feedback, clarification, and help, you can't
beat the power of a small, dedicated group focused on
mastering the task.

☑ Survival Tips:

1. **Form study groups after the first few classes.** Wait and see who the reliable students are before you join a group. Jumping in too soon might mean ending up with a less productive group. Be particularly observant about who does the homework, knows the answers, and seems to have a genuine interest in the class before you decide to form a study group.

2. **Keep the group number to a handful and make it diverse.** A group of three to five people is ideal. Two people are better than one, but three to five are much better than two. Groups of more than five make it too difficult to get together or make decisions. Also, vary the group by both gender and race because the diversity will make for a richer decision-making process.

3. **Vary personality types and include the professor's type.** What you want to avoid is having everyone in the group with the same personality type. If possible, try to have a person or two in the group with a personality similar to that of the professor. By having different personality styles in it, the small group becomes a more diverse critical test audience to use before launching new ideas.

4. **Meet at a regular time and place.** Setting both a time and place will ensure, above all else, that people will have something ready for the meeting. It's much like telling someone you'll go for a walk or meet them for lunch. You'll tend to do it if you've agreed on a time and place. Putting a study group in your schedule is the best way to make certain that you'll study. Block out your schedule and set your priorities.

5. **Be persistent.** Don't give up on the group. If at first you don't succeed, try, try again. Groups need to get comfortable with themselves. They need to establish trust and confidence. That comes only with time. Don't give up at the first sign of problems. Work through them with candor and caring for every member in the group. And always keep the objective in mind: To understand, to learn, and to help each other through the course.

Myth #5
I have plenty of time to finish the assignment.

"I'll look like a real nerd if I start studying too early."

"Lighten up. This is a long run."

"Chill out. I'll go out and unwind."

"I have better things to do."

"This is the perfect time to get to know everyone–before the workload picks up."

"College isn't just about studying; the social part may be more important."

Reality #5
Establish regular study habits from the start.

The first semester at any university is one of the most exciting and potentially one of the most dangerous times in your academic career, for several reasons.

- *You're away from home, in many cases for the first time.* Free at last to make your own decisions. That's both the good and bad news. Good news: You can do anything you want, whenever you want. Bad news: You can do anything you want, whenever you want. Granted, there are no nagging parental questions: "Did you get your homework done?" or even worse, "Let me see it." But while the nagging's gone, so is the pressure and help of oversight.

- *There's a ton of pressure to get to know everyone, right away.* Many roommates, suitemates, and classmates succumb to this pressure. Eventually, most recognize that this will not work unless they have nothing else to do.

- *You may not have anything specific that's due right away.* You don't have a paper or research project due for a month or two. So, it's tempting to sit back and enjoy the extended summer.

- *Fall is about the nicest season of the year.* Cool evenings and warm days–perfect for picnics, football, or just about anything you can think of. Studying does not rank up there with the coolest things to do on a beautiful autumn day.

In fact, you'd be hard pressed to find a single thing about the early part of your first-year first semester that makes studying attractive.

But the *reality* is that *not* starting early may mean failing later. Stuff just has a way of piling up on you. Here's a typical scenario: You let a few reading assignments slide and then you put a short paper or two on hold. Multiply the procrastination by five or six other "minor" assignments you also let slide and you're talking some serious pileup problems. And it all sneaks up on you very innocently.

✓ Survival Tips:

1. **Find the time of day you learn best–AM or PM.**
   Most people are either morning or night people.
   Determine which one you are and use that time to do
   the most important job you have while in school…
   surviving. To test whether you're a day or night person,
   ask yourself these questions: "Do I like waking up early
   and getting a start on the day?" If you answer "yes,"
   you're likely a morning person. So, set aside an hour or
   two every morning to hit the books. Schedule it ahead
   of time. Pay the study master first. If you answer "yes"
   to the question "Do I get going later in the afternoon or
   evening?" then you're most likely a night person; so set
   aside time in the evening to study. This gives
   information the best shot at sticking to your brain.

2. **Let your friends know that your study time is
   sacred.** While you may get some grief early on from
   people, as soon as they know you're serious, you'll get
   few, if any, invasions of your study time. People will
   actually respect that you say what you mean and mean
   what you say.

3. **Find a place to study.** Dormitories, especially first-year dorms, are notoriously bad places to study. Understand that and deal with it. Places like unused classrooms, library carousels, coffee shops, the back of an auditorium, a car–anywhere away from friends—will do. They may hassle you to see a movie, party, or just hang out. You can do that later. Hit the books first.

4. **Give yourself a break.** Just as scheduling regular study time contributes to success, so does taking a five to ten minute break every hour. Rest your eyes, wash your face…turn off the brain for a few minutes. Then get back to it. If you find yourself dozing off, stop where you are. Allow yourself to doze off–sitting up, not lying down. You'll find this "sitting doze" a form of meditation that increases alertness and concentration.

5. **Just do it**. The Nike commercial says: "Just Do It." I say we should adapt that to academic studies: "Just study it." Establishing the habit right away is key. The first day you have classes, find a place to study, and keep going there at your best study time, even when you think you're wasting your time. The routine of having a regular time and place to review your notes and read the required material will be more beneficial than you can imagine.

Myth #6
I don't need any help.

"If I keep studying, I'll get it."

"I'm smart, I'll figure it out."

"Only dumb people have tutors."

"What will others think if they know I'm getting tutored?"

"I'm cheating if I get my own private teacher."

"Something must be very wrong if I need that kind of help."

"I never needed to ask for help in the past."

Reality #6
Asking for help is smart, not stupid.

Most people are hung up on the idea of asking for help. From the time we're born, we are told that the American ethic is self-reliance. Pull your own weight, row your own boat, pull yourself up by your bootstraps, and a host of other similar sayings pervade our culture.

There's also a notion that if you reach out for help, you'll be labeled as abnormal, and we all know how important it is to be in the center of the bell curve. I've always been stunned by the irony of teenagers who strive for absolute autonomy and individuality as they separate from their parents, only to dress, speak, and act precisely as their peers do. They often go to extraordinary measures not to color outside the careful lines drawn by their peers. In short, if no one else is being tutored...it's not cool.

I remember when my daughter took statistics in college. She's a bright young woman who graduated with honors. But statistics nearly drove her nuts. She began to have that typical self-doubt and her confidence slipped. This is quite normal, but what she did was not. After consulting with the teacher, she decided that she needed extra instruction; so, she hired a tutor. She met with him quite regularly and salvaged her grade through hard work and determination.

If you still have doubts about the normalcy of tutors, think about Olympic and professional athletes. Can you possibly imagine any high-caliber athlete not having a private coach, at least periodically? Most private coaches travel with their athletes to be close by when trouble arises.

What about top-level musicians? Could you imagine them not having private, ongoing tutoring or teaching? They must have help to keep them sharp in an increasingly competitive world.

So, if tutors (coaches and private instructors) are good enough for the very best competitors in our country, don't you think we all should give them a try, especially when we're faltering a bit? Besides, many schools even offer tutoring free of charge.

☑ Survival Tips:

1. **Talk to the professor early in the semester.** You'll
   see this tip come up again and again because it's one of
   the best pieces of advice I can give. Don't wait until
   you're literally bailing out water from a sinking ship.
   Once you see some water seeping in, talk to the captain
   of the ship. Early is much better than later, but most
   students with problems wait too long to come in. And
   the first thing I or any other professor will say is,
   "Why'd you wait until now?" Many times, when
   students come in asking how they can salvage their
   grades, it's just too late.

2. **Ask for recommendations from the professor.** Often
   the professor will know who is a good tutor and who is
   not. Finding the right fit is vital, and often the professor
   can recommend the best graduate assistants and even
   undergrads who are most suited to help to you.

3. **Go to the student counseling office.** Most colleges
   have a counseling office that will help you find a tutor.
   Often they keep databases of tutors and their fees, and
   you can usually obtain a printout. Tutors' rates will vary
   depending on their expertise, but at least you'll get an
   idea of prices. Most universities have standard fees that
   tutors should charge; so, even if you go off campus for
   a tutor, you'll know the ballpark figures.

4. **Look at tutors as an investment, not an expense.**
   Don't get hung up on money. Tutors are among the best
   dollar-for-dollar investments you can make. Like
   private coaches, they speed up your recovery from
   problems and can provide stress relief. They may cost
   several hundreds of dollars, but the relief is worth
   thousands. However, let me say again: Many schools
   will offer free tutoring.

5. **Don't be afraid to change tutors if things don't work
   out.** Remember that tutors are people who have
   individual personalities and quirks that you might find
   annoying and whose teaching style is not productive for
   you. If so, move on to another tutor. Tutors provide a
   service and when the service is a liability, cut your
   losses. If you find this awkward to handle face to face,
   do it by e-mail or letter. Often an e-mail or letter with a
   follow-up phone call, at most, takes care of a tough
   situation. But don't continue to pay for a bad product or
   service.

Myth #7
I don't have to like a course to do well.

"This course sucks."

"This professor stinks."

"I'm entitled to my opinion."

"I'd rather have a dental filling than go to this class."

"I'm not learning a damned thing in that class."

"This is THE worst class I have ever taken."

"Why me?"

"I'll write letters to friends to occupy my time in class."

Reality #7
Attitude, not ability, will determine your success in college.

Some people will mightily disagree with me on the notion that you must like something to do well. OK. That's your opinion, and you're entitled to it! But my experience in a classroom is that students who have an "attitude" (a negative disposition) toward either the subject or the teacher do not perform as well as they should.

I have watched this "attitude" phenomenon for years. In fact, it's so prominent in required courses that you cannot miss it. The school tells students that they must take English 101 or Communication 101, and students resent it. It's human nature to rebel when someone says you *must* do it. In contrast, I find that in elective courses students have more of an interest and the results are dramatically different. They participate more in class, read the assignments, turn in higher quality materials, talk to the teacher more, and generally are more fun.

Don't think that intelligence (ability) will substitute for a good attitude, because it will not. Underline <u>NOT</u>. Being bright is a gift that many people squander because of a bad attitude. The world is chock full of half-baked geniuses, potential Olympic athletes, and superstar talents who never made it. Why? Because attitude, not ability, will determine your success.

Think about your own experiences. How many great potential athletes, students, workers have you seen come down the pike brimming with the ability—the aptitude—but whose attitude was impoverished? The results are always the same: Excuses. "I would have...could have... should have." "That damned coach hates me." "That instructor doesn't like the way I dress." The list goes on. You've heard it over and over by those who fail to reach their altitude...usually because of their attitude.

✅ Survival Tips:

1. **Think like an advertiser.** In advertising, the first thing the ad must do is tell the customers how the product or service will benefit them. Otherwise, it's nearly impossible to sell anything. Therefore, find the benefit to you by looking at the syllabus and discovering two or three issues that you find interesting. Focus on those for starters. Other benefits will follow.

2. **Look for long-term, not short-term, benefits.** As you begin to look for benefits, beware of shortsightedness. Students tend to look for instant gratification–what's in it for me…right this very second in my life. This will disappoint you because it's difficult to see how Columbus' rationale for exploration in 1492 has any direct, immediate impact on your life. Rather than this myopic stance, take the long view to learning. Ask yourself, "What can history teach me?" "Will understanding the why's help me understand the what's?" The answer is absolutely YES. What you learn in college helps prepare you to think through important issues and apply them to your daily life.

3. **Act like a baby-sitter.** Pretend that you're counseling a younger brother or sister about a particular class and you sense a negative attitude. You want to tell them how important such a course is and why it should be

taken seriously. What advice would you give ? I discovered this approach when I was about 12 years old and was baby-sitting for our neighbor's kids. One day I started lecturing the kids about picking up their clothes and putting toys away. As I did, I began to sound like my own parents. Horrors. When I got home, I immediately cleaned my own room. My mother nearly fainted. By giving someone else good, solid advice, you teach yourself.

4. **Remember the Tortoise and the Hare.** This is a corny story that you no doubt have heard since you were a child. But it is right on the money. The two, as you recall, were in a race. The hare should have won hands down, no sweat. But he took his talent (aptitude) for granted and underestimated a competitor with great attitude. Attitude beats aptitude every time.

5. **Avoid making negative comments about the course or the professor.** A philosopher once heard a man speaking poorly about another man in public. The philosopher stopped the speaker and admonished him not to say such damaging things about another. The speaker asked the philosopher if he was trying to protect the man who was the subject of the negative comments. "No," said the philosopher calmly, "I was trying to protect you from yourself."

Negative comments about people can become self-destructive. Take this to the bank. Making and repeating comments begins to program your thinking for good or bad. When you start down this negative path it's pretty hard to get back. I've seen students develop an "attitude" and then try to defend it long after everyone else has seen that it no longer makes sense. Keep your comments positive–they foster a positive attitude.

Myth #8
It's better to drop a course rather than to risk a low grade.

"I just can't make it."

"No way I'm going to pass this class."

"This guy's the toughest professor I've ever had."

"She'll never give me a passing grade."

"I'm just not as smart as these brains."

"I don't have the background to survive in this course."

"This one's way over my head."

Reality #8
Never give up on a course too quickly.

Oftentimes you think you're being smart to cut your losses. But, if you've followed the other survival tips in this book, then I say never give up. Chances are better than even that if you've done your best, shown the professor you care, and all the rest—you'll make it through. But I constantly hear of students wanting to drop courses for all sorts of reasons: fear, self-doubt, laziness, poor scheduling, and so on.

The Chinese symbol for crisis has two characters: One means danger and the other opportunity. This is precisely where students who want to drop a class stand: on the horns of opposing solutions.

First, let's take danger. Despite your best efforts, you're in a course doing poorly. Things don't look good. You're going to class, doing the work, but your performance in tests and papers is not meeting your expectations. Your professor is supportive, but no pushover. Looks like piles and piles of work to pull this one out. Danger with a capital "D" lurks about. So you think that maybe it's time to drop it.

Second, let's look at opportunity. Most teachers reward those who persevere. They actually do give (though sometimes invisible) points for effort. Everyone likes the student who keeps plugging away. I once got a "C" in a college German class because the professor called me a hard worker and a morale booster–I was amusing. According to my calculations, I should have gotten a "D," but I studied hard, hung in there, and entertained the class and professor, especially with my imitations of both a deep southerner and a Yankee pronouncing classic German.

Professors almost always curve the grades at the end of the semester, though many will deny it. The fact is that most teachers can't afford to have two-thirds of the class do poorly. It doesn't reflect well on the professor's competence.

So, here's my simple advice: Hang in there. Do your best and follow the other advice in this book. If you do that, you'll survive any course and any professor.

✔ Survival Tips:

1. **Don't be afraid of the professor.** Often upperclass students will tell wild tales about certain professors whose reputations become legendary, even mythical. Before entering the classroom, students are many times so overwhelmed by this reputation that they convince themselves that they can't possibly score an "A." Despite the stereotypes, most professors are "been there, done that" types. They have all bombed classes, experimented with life and its various detractors, and been in exactly the same position you're in now. Talk to them. Get their advice about whether it's wise for you to drop or not. Mostly, from my experience, I think they'll tell you to hang in there. Listen to them.

2. **Believe in yourself.** Most of life's successes depend on confidence. In college, you can underline that. If you think you can—you will. If you think you can't—you won't. The best way to develop self-confidence is to think of the many things you've accomplished in the past that you might have had doubts about when you first began. I've found that discussing with students the toughest thing they've ever learned, and how they overcame their fear and doubt, works very well. They begin to see how even learning to drive a car was daunting at first, but with practice—even a few accidents—they began to believe in themselves.

3. **Check your assumptions.** Sometimes you think, "What's the use? I'm already flunking." Maybe, maybe not. Get to the professor as soon as possible and ask how well you're doing. You may be shocked to find out that you're doing about the same as others in the class even though you think you're about to be shot at dawn. Don't assume anything.

4. **Benchmark with other students.** Benchmarking is what corporations do all the time to tell how they're doing. They look at the other companies' products and services and compare their own. Sometimes they find that they're better, other times they find they're worse. In either case, it helps to know where you stand. Do that with fellow students. You'll often find that you're doing better than you think. Somehow this kind of check always gave me courage to plow ahead.

5. **Quitters never win, and winners never quit.** I know this sounds like another bumper sticker, but I believe it. Hanging in there is one of life's great lessons. There are a lot of ventures that you'll begin in your life and will want to quit early on, thinking, "I'll never get through this one." Learn to face that self-doubt bogeyman now because he will not go away.

Myth #9
If you don't succeed, it's not for you.

"I can't do it."

"I got an F on the first test. That's it for me."

"I'm going to join the Army."

"I was not cut out for this."

"I'll never recover from the first semester grades."

"I'm ashamed. That's it. I quit."

"I knew I couldn't do it."

"I never was all that hot on college anyway."

Reality #9
Important lessons are learned from failures.

The most difficult semester for me was my first year of college, first semester. I had been an honor student in high school. Then came college and pre-med classes. I found myself on the lower half of the grade scale and decided to quit school and join the Marines. I even moved my clothes out during winter break to avoid embarrassing myself with my roommates. During the break, I met a U.S. Marine who, to my surprise, discouraged me from joining up until I finished school. He probably was the best college counselor I ever had.

I didn't quit; I learned. I moved my stuff back into the dorm before my roommates returned, finished out the year, changed my major to English, graduated, and later went into the U.S. Marine Corps as an officer.

My story is not unique. Ask your parents or older friends who have gone to college, and you'll hear something similar. The message is simple. Hang in there and learn from the inevitable failures in college and in life. It's not the failure that's the big deal; it's how you respond and learn from it. If you keep making the same mistake over and over again, like the cartoon of the coyote chasing the roadrunner, then you need to think about a new planet to live on. But, if you learn and grow, you've discovered the essence of this thing called life.

A conventional piece of wisdom says that most successful business people fail at least three times in their careers. That's because in order to be successful, you have to stretch, work outside your comfort zone, and take risks. Risks are scary, but they also provide opportunities. So, if you're to be successful, you'll be taking risks. Some ventures will fail–that's the nature of the beast. Learn and for goodness sake, don't stop taking risks.

✅ Survival Tips:

1. **Learn, don't burn.** When you fail, learn from it by asking yourself why it happened. Was it a scheduling problem or something more fundamental like your writing or reading skills? The worst thing to do is sit in your room stewing about the course, the professor, your roommate, or the stars. Often when faced with a failure, people blame virtually everybody and everything else rather than face up to the fact that they alone are responsible.

2. **Don't be afraid to change your major.** Don't do this lightly or without consulting people who care, but also don't be afraid to do it if you find a significant mismatch between you and your major. Remember how most majors are picked. It's Saturday night, you meet an attractive person, and you ask about his or her major. The rapport is growing. The next day you're an archaeology major–although yesterday you didn't know what it was, and you couldn't even spell it. Given this highly analytical selection process, don't be overly invested in that major. In this case, failure may just be an intelligent redirection.

3. **Keep a sense of humor.** Above all things in college, as in life, keep your sense of humor and start by laughing at yourself. You'll always have a good laugh, and self-

deprecation is great humor for others as well. Failure can make us all deadly serious, as if our actions would change the course of generations to come. Get over it. Look at a misstep with humor. Joke about it, as you learn from it. For your own health, learn to laugh. In fact, many studies over the years have conclusively demonstrated that laughter is the best medicine. Rent a bunch of comedies your first year. That's the best way I know to get a quick laugh when I'm not feeling great about a recent failure.

4. **Remember that great people fail.** Great men and women experience failure. They lose elections, fall from grace. History is chock full of them. My uncle Joe is a great businessman who's had a bunch of successes and failures in his life. I think that's what makes him successful. In fact there's an old saying, "What doesn't kill you makes you stronger." In my experience, I've found that to be true.

5. **You can't please everyone.** One sure formula for failure is trying to please everyone around you. You have to define life and success for yourself. For some who are physically challenged, success is getting up in the morning and being able to function independently. For great athletes it might mean running a four-minute mile. The definition of failure and success varies, and it's all relative. Keep yourself as the focus when drawing those boundaries.

Myth #10
I don't have enough experience to trust myself.

"Hey, I'm only a kid."

"I just graduated from high school."

"I'm allowed to make a certain number of errors."

"I'm in college, I'm supposed to experiment."

"Everybody is doing it."

"They'll think I'm a jerk if I don't do it."

"If it doesn't hurt anyone else, what's wrong with it?"

"If I ask, I'll look stupid."

Reality #10
Listen to your instincts.

Your instincts and judgment got you this far–to college. They can take you through college as well. There's a tremendous freedom that comes with leaving for college. The release from nagging (and loving) parents, getting to leave your dirty laundry on the floor for weeks at a time, eating what and when you want, and a raft of other new-found freedoms are exhilarating. That's the good news.

But the bad news is that you're now responsible for what you do. Remember, at age 18 you're now not just personally but legally responsible for your actions. This has great implications. You can vote, but you can also be arrested and tried as an adult. You can sign for credit cards, but you can be sued for non-payment. The lists of rights and responsibilities are enormous, and the choices are all yours to make.

In fact, the idea of independence is all about choices–both good and bad. I grew up in a poor neighborhood. Most of us had about the same amount of money (very little) and the same types of choices. Several kids in my old neighborhood went to jail. Others went on to be professionals and became quite successful. What made much of the difference were the choices people made.

Choice is a wide-open proposition, and it's a dilemma for most of us. I once heard a forensic psychiatrist talk about the criminally insane. As a psychiatrist at a major psychiatric hospital who had seen over 5,000 criminally insane patients in his career, he reached the conclusion that doing wrong is a conscious act. Based on thousands of patient interviews, he had unequivocally concluded that doing right or wrong was a choice. I'll never forget the force with which he delivered that point to a group of police officers, and his follow-up message was clear: Don't spend any time feeling sorry for those who make such choices when they get arrested.

College is full of choices—some good, some bad. The choices abound: To study or not; to drink and drive or not; to cheat or not. My message to you is a takeoff on what the psychiatrist said: Don't do something unless you're pre-pared for the consequences of your actions. Or as police officers say, "Don't do the crime, if you can't do the time."

☑ Survival Tips:

1. **Figure out how you make your best decisions**. Most people decide either with their heads or their hearts. "Head" types decide based on the logic and the arguments for and against doing something much like a lawyer might. They weigh both sides of an issue and even internally argue both sides. Whichever seems the stronger of the two arguments wins. Often the outcome is much like a court case: one side wins and the other loses. "Heart" types tend to use their gut as a basis to react to issues. They rely much more on their basic gut reactions to situations as a barometer. If things feel right, then this type of person can be assured that chances are good they're making the right decision. Both head and heart decision makers are very good at the process if they rely on their distinctive strengths.

2. **Test your decision with those who think differently than you.** When you're about to decide on an issue that's important to you, get some counterpoint views from people who don't think like you. It's always better to test your ideas among friends and relatives before you expose your decision to the scrutiny of the world. It's much less painful; much more constructive.

3. **Use the red-face test.** When faced with the many types and sizes of decisions you'll likely have to make in college, I highly recommend the red-face technique. Ask yourself this one basic question: If I did this thing I'm about to do, and it was reported on the front page of my local newspaper or put on the evening news, would I be embarrassed? If the answer is yes...then don't just walk from the situation, run from it. You'll be glad you did.

4. **Find a sounding board.** Everyone needs someone to listen to them. I once heard that psychiatrists and psychologists get about a 50 percent cure rate but that people who have a good friend they can talk to are cured at a rate over 70 percent. My memory of those numbers might be off a couple of points, but the message that the report sent was clear: A good sounding board is vital to your mental health. Find one.

5. **When you make a bad decision, learn from it**. Notice that I said, "when," not "if" you make a bad decision. Bad decisions are as much a part of life as breathing. Most people would "revise" some decisions in their lives, given the opportunity. The key is not that you make a bad decision here or there, but that you learn from it. You should mature from the experience.

Conclusion

By now your eyes may be glazed over from all this advice. Make no mistake, I did not always follow my own advice, nor did most of your parents. So, if you toss this book in the trash can and need **one** piece of advice to live by, try this: Ask yourself what advice you'd give to younger sisters or brothers if they were in your place. Then listen to that voice…it's the voice of objective experience. Hopefully I was able to give some of that to you. Certainly, your parents have tried to do that as well.

In closing, let me leave you with this simple thumbnail list of realities:

1. Train early
2. Attend all classes
3. Study the professor
4. Form study groups
5. Establish regular study habits
6. Ask for help
7. Develop a positive attitude
8. Never give up too quickly
9. Learn from failure
10. Listen to your instincts

I wish you the best of luck as you find your own path navigating the first year of college.